If
Quilts
Could
Talk

My Quilts, My Stories
Volume 1

by

Aisha Lumumba

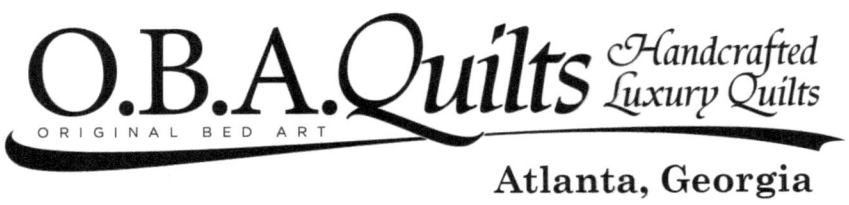

Atlanta, Georgia

ISBN 13: 978-0-9639594-5-4
ISBN 10: 0-9639594-5-X

Photography: Aisha and Jabari Lumumba

Acknowledgement

"The joy that isn't shared dies young."
~Anne Sexton

Over the past 5 years, I have promised that this book would be published soon. I would like to thank all the people who enjoyed my short stories as they were developing. Thanks to Jerry G. White for my first reading engagement during the Decatur Arts Festival, and the wonderful people at the National Black Arts Festival where I did a storytelling presentation. Thanks to the Episcopal Church Women (ECW) at the Episcopal Church Of Saint John & Saint Mark in Albany, Georgia, who invited me to their Annual Women's Tea, the Decatur Public Library, the Eagles Landing High School for inviting me to their Black History Month Program, Peach State Stitchers/Pomegranate Guild and the many people who came to my exhibits to hear these stories.

I would not be able to write without the unending support and help of my spouse, Chinyelu Lumumba. I am forever grateful for his patience. The support of my entire family (immediate and extended) is so overwhelmingly wonderful that I could not name them all here but they are all included in my gratitude.

I'd like to thank Jabari Lumumba for his great photography. Extreme gratitude goes to Sharifa Lumumba and Jamal Pope for the expert graphic support and advice. Thanks to J. Stacey Grayson, Cynthia P. Laster, Clara P. Wright, Mary E. Sirmans Johnson, and Sharifa Lumumba for keeping my words on the right path. Many thanks to Malaika and Anane Lumumba for the greatest marketing ideas and help ever.

Appreciation and much gratitude to Kyra Hicks for writing **How To Self-Publish Your Own Quilt Catalog**. Her book continues to inspire me to publish more. I'd also like to give a super special thanks to Jahsasamut M. Watson for her insight and spontaneous cleverness.

I have some really good friends who are always here even when they are away doing other things. I thank them all. To many of those friends from my childhood that grace these stories, thanks and love.

Table of Contents

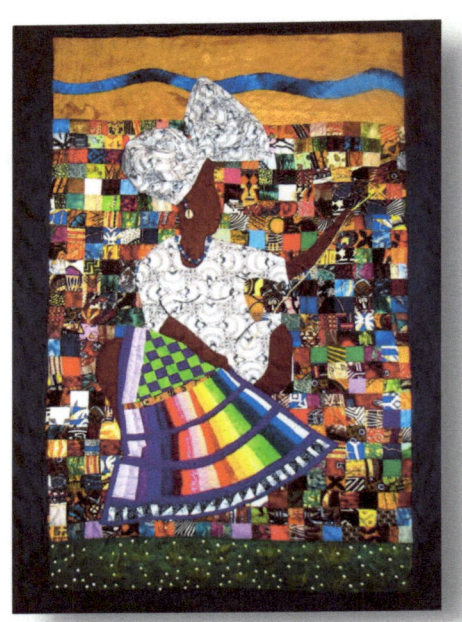

A Quilter's Dream is to be One with the Quilt
2010

Introduction

It has always been my contention that if my quilts could talk, they would sing the blues. I love the blues, but I think it is one of the most misunderstood forms of music. Most people think that blues songs are just about sadness. I say, think of it as just plain good music that tries to explore human emotions through sound. It's about loves, losses and passions. It is music that strives to find that special note. The artists call it the *"blue"* note - that forgotten note that strikes a chord inside your being; that misunderstood note that lets you feel the depth of the song while swaying to the music; that private note that you have shared ly with God. Most blues singers want you to go through the feelings i come out on the other side feeling better. My quilts are fabric ries that render to touch and sight, those kinds of blues.

rive to create a work of art that strikes that blue chord inside to help heal. Life is filled with bitter-sweet moments. It's difficult to sidestep r sad situations and we often find them intertwined with happy ies, kind of like the blues. I want harmony of colors and design to rate in the heart of the viewer, to feel the vibrations as they release ound. Oh yes! My quilts vibrate that blues sound.

a personal testimony, I enjoy and can engage in many varied endeav- , sometimes too many to keep focus (oh, the burdens of a creative ul). In my latter years, I have finally narrowed it down to two ssions: the love of sewing and the love of writing.

Iy sewing journey began when I found my mother's old treadle sewing achine in the corner of the back room. In my deepest spirit, I knew ow to sew right away and only needed instruction in the details of roper machine techniques. My brother, Galvin, came to the rescue and aught me to thread it correctly. With his help, the assistance of my Aunt Marie and some fantastic Home Economics teachers employed at Henry County (Georgia) Training School, I learned the art of sewing. I saved fabric scraps for years with the idea in mind that one day I would make a quilt. Then one day out of the blue, the quilting bug just bit me. The rest is history.

My writing journey began in elementary school. I vividly remember going to school that fall and having the first writing assignment-"How I Spent My Summer Vacation." I was so embarrassed. My sister and I had basically done nothing for the summer, or so I naively thought.

We simply chased bugs and ran barefoot through the grass and on unpaved dirt roads. "No one would want to hear about that," I thought. I wanted to tell stories about fantastic adventures and exotic travels; about going to a faraway place to visit a parent who no longer lived with me, about going shopping in fabulous, big-city department stores to buy "store-bought" things. I felt I had nothing, had done nothing, and had nothing to share.

If I had only appreciated the gleam in my sister's eyes when we saw an elusive butterfly, I could have written beautiful stories about that. Or could have written revealing prose about my older sister pining for her husband in Vietnam while playing "Wait A Minute Mr. Postman" over, and over, and over on the record player. I could have written an insightful piece about a trip to Atlanta in the back seat of my father's car. My sister, Cynthia and I begged and pleaded for him to stop at the brand new Dairy Queen to get ice cream cones. He didn't have the heart to tell us that they wouldn't serve us ice cream because of the color of our skin. Instead, he let us think that he was just a mean, ole' man that didn't want his cute little girls- the loves of his life- to have any ice cream. Many of my childhood memories could have been fuel for remarkable stories, but I didn't know that then.

After writing my first book, **Afterwhile**, I was bombarded with questions about my favorite author. I would say it was (still is) Zora Neale Hurston, hands down! Of course, I loved what she wrote but my admiration was centered on *how* she wrote. Certainly, she is more difficult than the average writer to read, but well worth the struggle. That style of dialectical writing is an important facet of our historical evolution here. As Eli Leon so elegantly wrote in his book **Accidentally On Purpose** about our language, "The language they (enslaved Africans) developed ultimately became 'Black English'- a dialect more disfavored in the larger society, perhaps, than any other in the history of English."

I declare that it was with great strength that she wrote in dialect when all the well-known scholars of her race at that time were denigrating that form of speech. She was not ashamed that we murdered the r's, turned the th's to d's, used double negatives, slurred words together to make new words that were more expressive for us and even mixed in a few words recalled from our home languages in Africa. We were searching for a rhythm. Our African languages had a different rhythm from

6

the English we were learning. So we dropped consonants and added syllables. Zora captured that rhythm in prose.

Over time we've had to stamp that rhythm out in order to survive, but when we get home among the closest of family and community, we drop the formalities. We speak Patois. We speak Geechee. We speak a little bit country. And yes, we even speak Ebonics. We speak our rhythms in our rhymes, our rhythms in our broadness, our rhythms in our rejection, and our rhythms in our blues. I have dared to be proud of a people who spoke at least two languages and were still considered "ignorant." I bring that **"only in the home"** rhythm to prose with my stories and through my quilts.

As you turn these pages, it is my prayer that you hear my voice speaking boldly to you, a voice that was almost silenced by the stress of life and lack of identity. I want you to feel as though I am sitting with you, telling you my stories over a hot cup of steaming tea or a bowl of home-made ice cream. I want you to feel comfortable enough to invite my book into your home, onto your bookshelves and coffee tables, and into your life. Once I'm in, it is my plan to enchant you with stories I once thought were not worthy of telling.

Oh, if quilts could talk... or sing the blues...

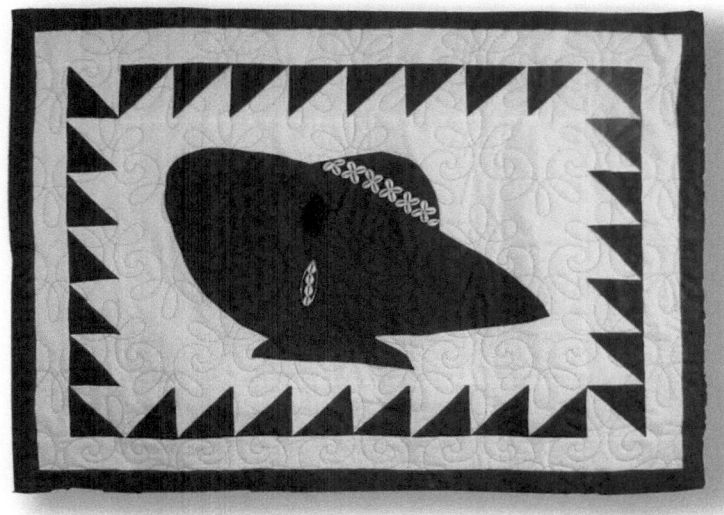

Mrs. Big #6
2006

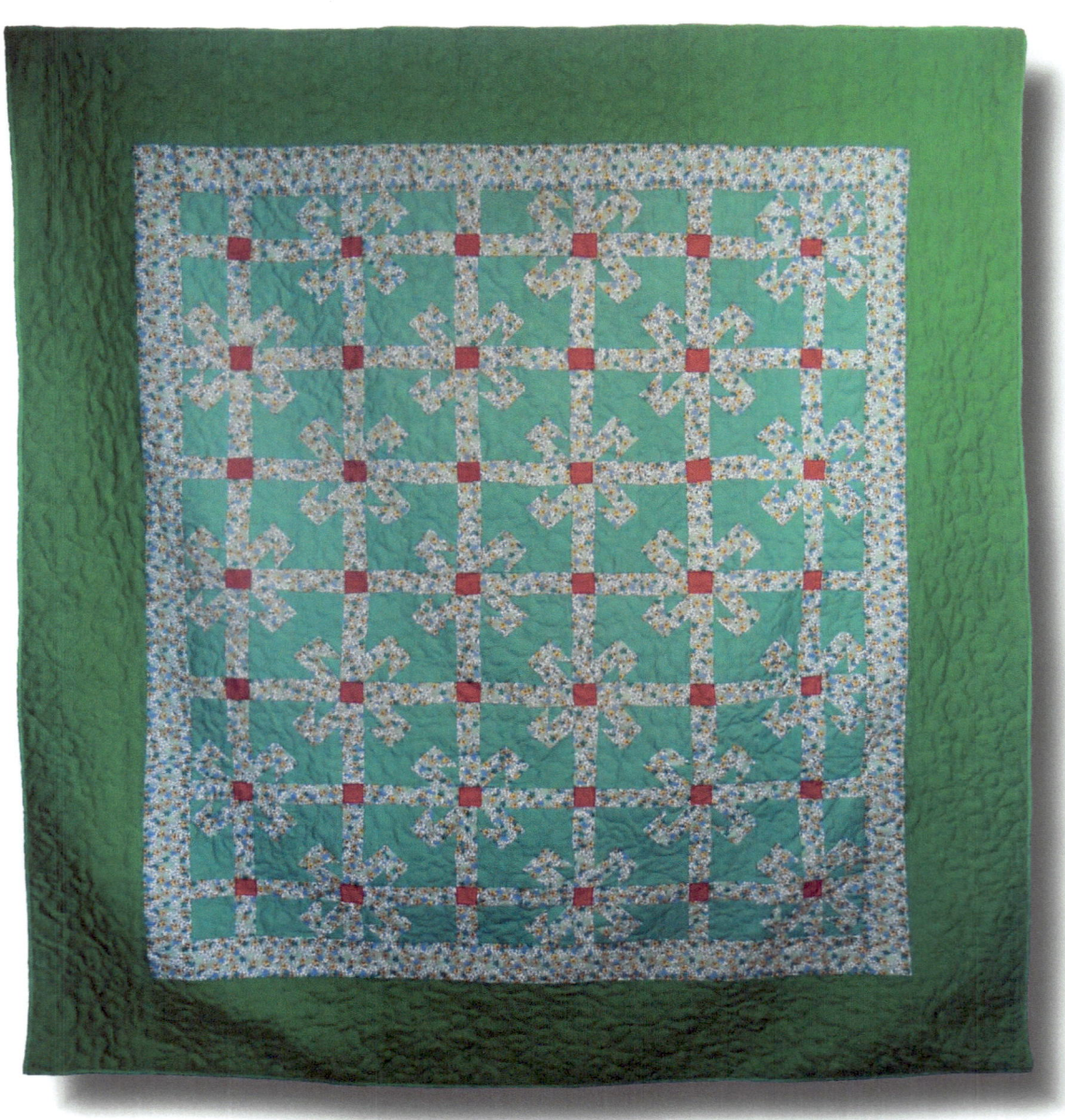

A Day Late and A Dollar Short
78" x 87"
2006

A Day Late and A Dollar Short

I could tell by the look in my father's eyes that he didn't think I could make this quilt. Back then, I couldn't understand why he thought that. I was an accomplished seamstress making men's suits and women's outfits. Then he put that look aside and let a smile come through as he beamed with pride about the two little pieces I had completed. He held them up and said, "I can see it on my bed now."

As children, our little inquisitive minds roamed outside in all seasons. We knew that the first sign of daffodils warned of impending spring-well really spring cleaning. An army of thorough cleaners swept through our home. Floors scrubbed, mattresses turned, quilts washed and flung on the line. Little did we know that we were washing away an important part of our history in baths of bleach and lye soap.

We always had quilts to keep us warm on cold winter nights after the fire died or the gas heater was turned off. Quilts were always there and always expected to be there; a necessity not art. Everybody made them- my grandmothers, my mother, my aunts and all the neighbors. I guess that's why quilts have a sacred place in my memory.

In my studies I found a quilt historian who said early quilts were not made of discarded fabrics and clothes. Well, she obviously did not do any research in my neighborhood. The quilts in our house were made from men's old suits and clothes that were no longer useful, and boy were they heavy. They pressed our little bodies down in the bed at night. Four or five of us in that bed, didn't have to worry about nobody rolling over. No need for them to be so heavy now. We have central heat in insulated houses to keep us warm.

9

Quilts often precipitated an avenue for social gathering. My friend Chekesha told me about her grandmother sitting at a large quilting frame. Chekesha's grandmother's friends would appear, pull up a chair and help with the quilt. The ladies were not only quilting but also talking and socializing. Chekesha's eyes watered as she remembered that the gatherings could only take place during the daylight hours because they had no electric lights.

My life was going along just fine. Then... Change came. He moved right into our house and took up permanent residence with our family. People living in the country often welcomed strangers, but Change would prove to be one we wish we had never seen. He was a dapper dresser, my father said. I looked up at his fancy suit with wide eyed amazement. My mother's untimely death was his first big move. It left a big chill in our family that only time could warm, but Aunt Marie's quilts supplied us with some relief.

Then the sewing muse became my best friend when I was six. I was fascinated with fabrics, colors and textures. My father brought fabrics for Aunt Marie's creations from the warehouse where he worked. He gave her bundles of scraps to make quilts and gave me a few to make doll clothes.

When I embarked on my first quilt project, I asked for my own bundle of scraps. My dad was so proud that I was interested in making quilts. He knew something about the dying art that I didn't. At age eighteen, I simply looked at one of the quilts, cut out the pieces and began to make it. I knew I could do it because I had seen it done so many times.

Quilting caught my attention but Life had some different ideas for my time. I got so busy building a life and raising my family that quilting drifted out of my mind. The quilt I started at eighteen was placed in a bag and forgotten. Here's where my thinking went wrong. Since I was making it for my father, there was plenty of time to get to it, I thought. I kept sewing over the years and saving scraps with the idea of one day making quilts. When I got married, my husband and I visited his grandmother often. Mother (we affectionately called her) showed me her many quilt projects and told me long stories about the fabrics. She reminded me that I had once tried to quilt.

At twenty-six, I picked up quilting again to pass the time during pregnancy. I found hand piecing to be soothing. I could put my body on automatic pilot and let my mind drift away to wonderful places and deep thoughts. My husband said, "Why don't you use the sewing machine to put together all those little pieces of fabric?" I like doing it this way, I'd reply. He would throw his hands in the air with frustration. Then shake his head that I had certainly lost my mind and leave me to my "little pieces of fabric."

Then the magic happened. I passed along the love of sewing. My first daughter, Malaika's eyes mirrored my fascination with it. She made her first quilt at age eight for her new baby sister Sharifa. Then, Sharifa made me proud when at age eighteen she made a quilt for her college dorm room. My youngest daughter, Anane hasn't decided to quilt yet, but I'm sure she will. My son may never quilt.

The quilts of my childhood were a faded memory. Then Change reared his head from the back corner and said, "Hey, I'm still here." I believed him too, because things were surely changing all around. Our children had grown up in the blink of an eye. The cost of everything had quadrupled and gray hairs were showing up in my own head. Then Change made another big move. I got the call that my father had died. It had never dawned on me that his time was drawing near. I thought I had all the time in the world and he'd always be there when I got back to him.

As time passed, I searched for that old bag of quilt scraps, partly pieced and waiting for me. I heard that quilts tell stories. When I looked at quilts I didn't hear stories, but it was because I hadn't learned to listen in that special way. I looked over the stitches that my young hands made before I really knew anything about quilting. It spoke history to me. It was made of pieces of fabric swept up by a man, my father, who worked his way from Janitor sweeping up scraps of fabric and other trash to Head Shipping Clerk; only to train the boss's eighteen-year-old son to be his supervisor. My father made $40.00 a week in his prime and spent it raising seven children alone. It spoke of my impetuousness at eighteen embarking on a project far beyond my years. The quilt spoke of twenty something years of neglect imposed on that bag of scraps as well as my father. Where had I been and where had the years gone? Will others be able to hear the history that my quilt speaks?

I will tell them. I will tell my grandchildren about these fabrics that were cousins to hospital scrub suits and nurse's smocks. I will tell them about a man that I called Daddy, my children called Granddaddy and they can certainly call Great Granddaddy. A caring man who worked hard to make a better world for his children than he'd experienced; a revolutionary man who fought disenfranchisement with all the available tools of his day; a loving man who helped other people with all the resources he could muster. It was late in my life before I realized my Daddy's greatness and extraordinary love. As a matter of fact it was too late, too late to tell him so, too late to give him this quilt. I was a day late and a dollar short.

On cold winter nights as the wind whistles past our windows, I wish my Dad were coming home from the plant to kiss me on the forehead and tuck me in. I wrap myself in his quilt and fall asleep remembering.

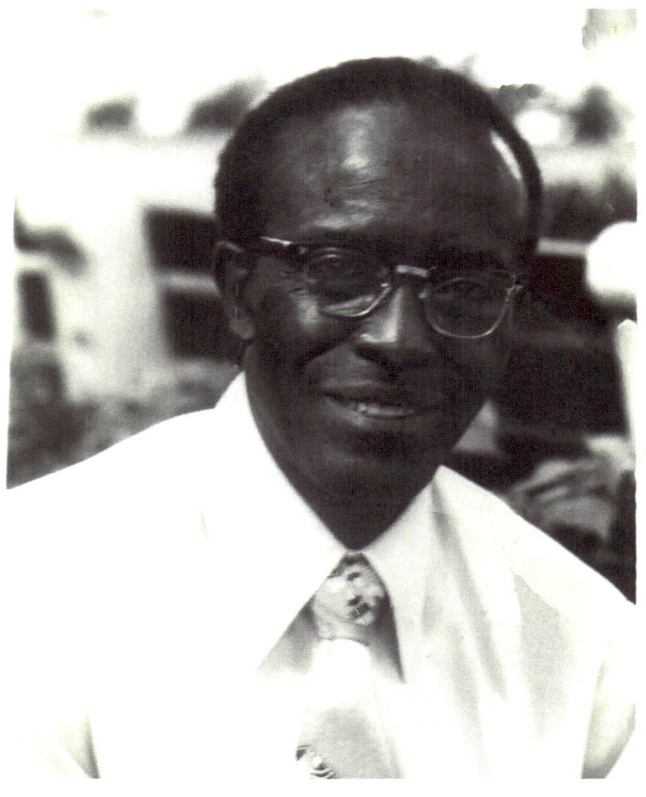

Joe D. Ponder

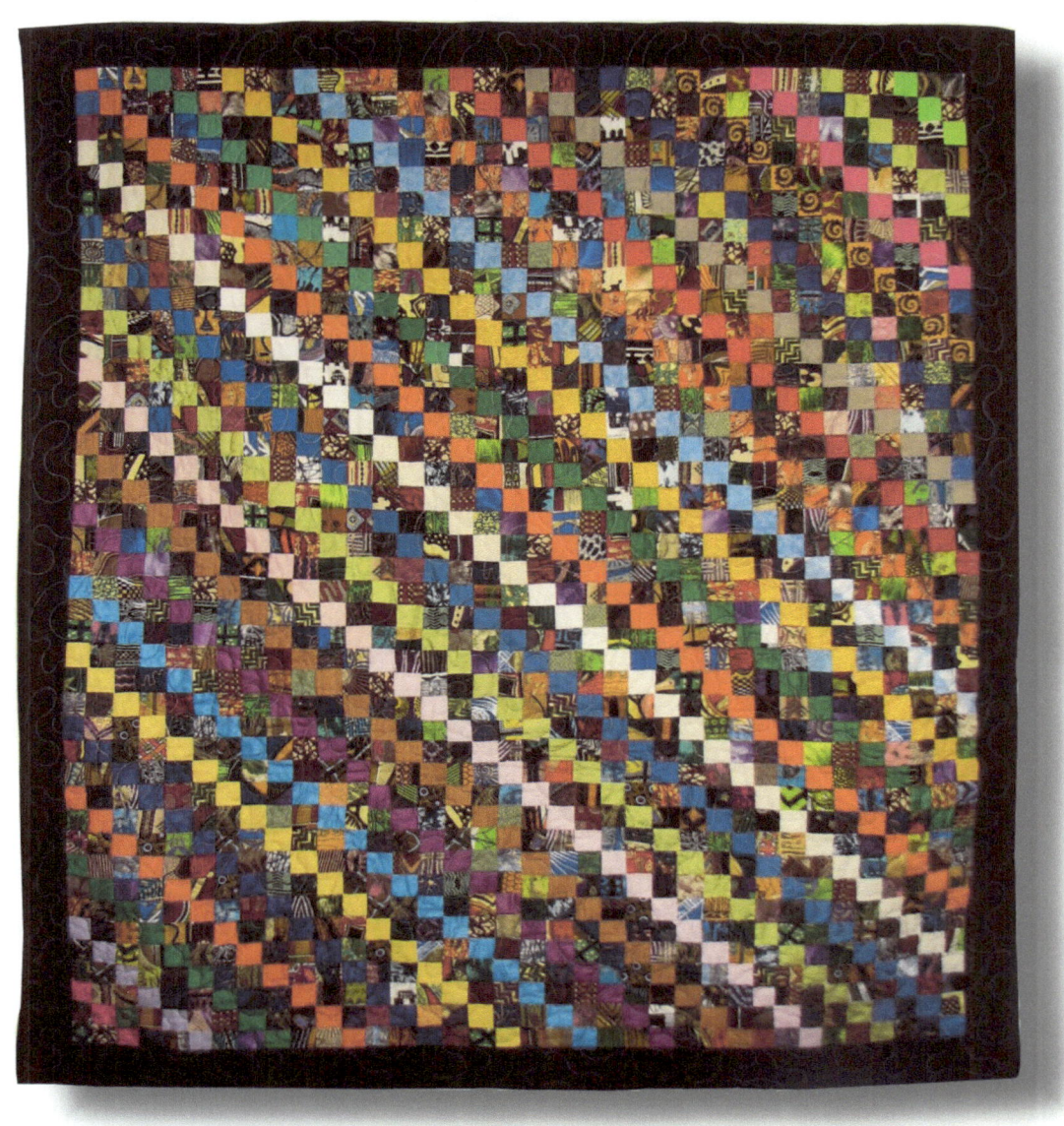

Tag #3
58" x 66"
2006

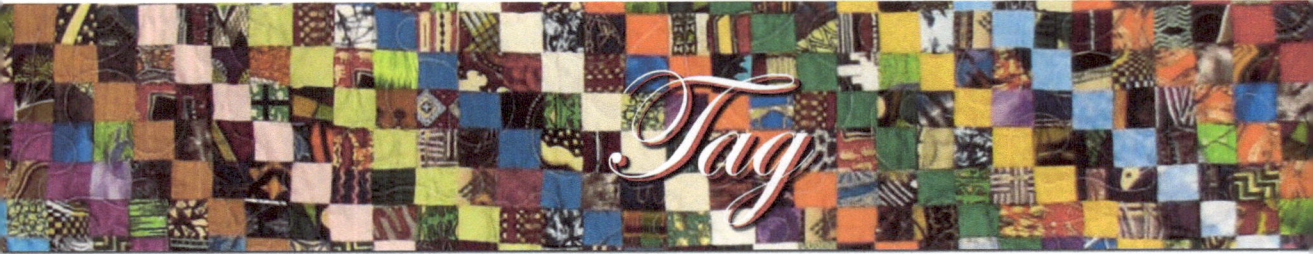

Tag

The best memories of my childhood are of playing day in and day out with my sister Cynthia. When we woke up in the morning, our main goal was to play until sunset. Most days we accomplished just that.

"I saw a June bug today," I said to my sister Cynthia. Her eyes sparkled at the thought. We couldn't tell time yet and surely didn't know which season followed which, but we knew what June bugs meant. June bugs meant playing outside with no shoes, such freedom. They meant that Wanda was coming to visit her great grandmother, Mama Lottie. Ms. Lottie lived next door and provided Cynthia and I with much curiosity. We knew our friend Wanda's coming was fun waiting to happen. We also knew that our cousins would be in town soon for the annual family gathering. We always gathered for my grandmother's birthday in June. Family gatherings meant dodge ball in the field with all my cousins, Aunt Bert's macaroni and cheese and Aunt Annie's pound cake. Yep, this time of the year meant fun and lots of it.

In between all those landmark occasions, Cynthia and I just made up our own fun. Some nights we caught June bugs and tied strings to their legs. They were kites for us. Children can be cruel in their pursuit of knowledge. We were surrounded with flowers that added to our fun. We would wake up early to snap the Morning Glories on the fence before they bloomed and before Ms. Lottie caught us. She needed those flowers so the bees would cross pollinate her garden. One day we decided to find out why Four O'clocks were called Four O'clocks. We must have asked our sister LaVern the time about one hundred times. The beautiful little red flowers did absolutely nothing at 4:00. Then there was the buttercup with that wonderful yellow center full of pollen. The thrill of our days was to trick someone, anyone into smelling the flower so we could smash it on their nose. It would leave a yellow dot right on the tip of the nose. We'd laugh for awhile.

It was the length of the warmer days that gave us time to chase June bugs, fireflies, bumble bees, plums, black berries, humming birds and each other. There was nothing more exhilarating than a good game of tag, especially when I was winning.

The weather got hotter and our lazy days were spent pretending to be Batman and Robin while jumping out of the pine trees with a blanket tied around our necks, but sunset brought the real excitement. The sun began to fade and the sky turned from pink to orange. The sound of crickets signaled dusk and as the orange sky faded, we would see the flicker of little gold lights. Off we'd run with outstretched hands to catch one of those little sparkles. Many times the lightning bugs were maimed in our little hands. By the time we'd filled a jar with our smelly little fireflies, we still had lots of energy to burn.

As I put the jar of fireflies on the porch. Cynthia would slip up behind me. Then I'd feel a tap at the same time I heard the words, "Tag, you're it!"

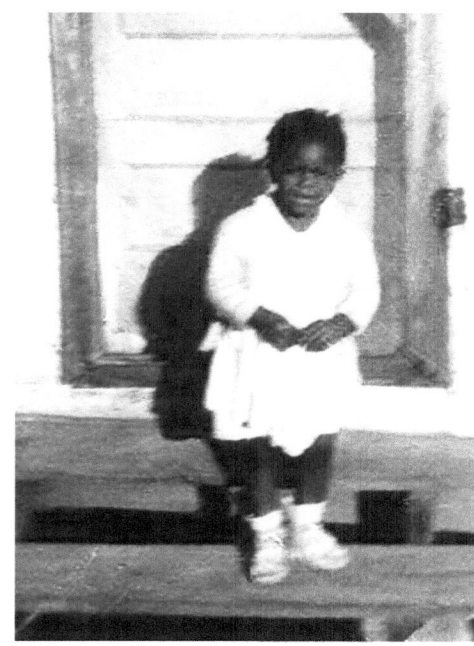

Aisha
Lumumba

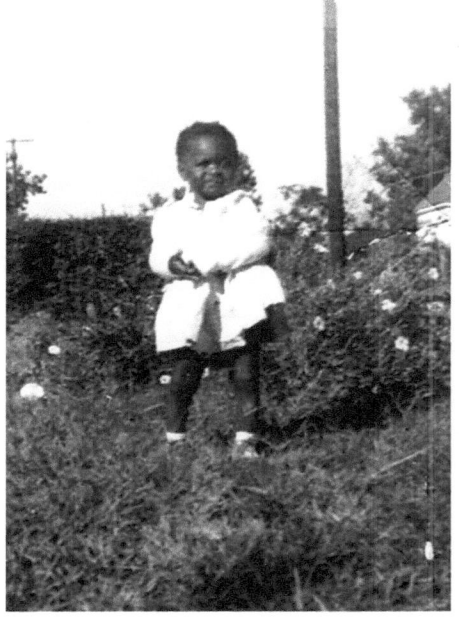

Cynthia P.
Laster

15

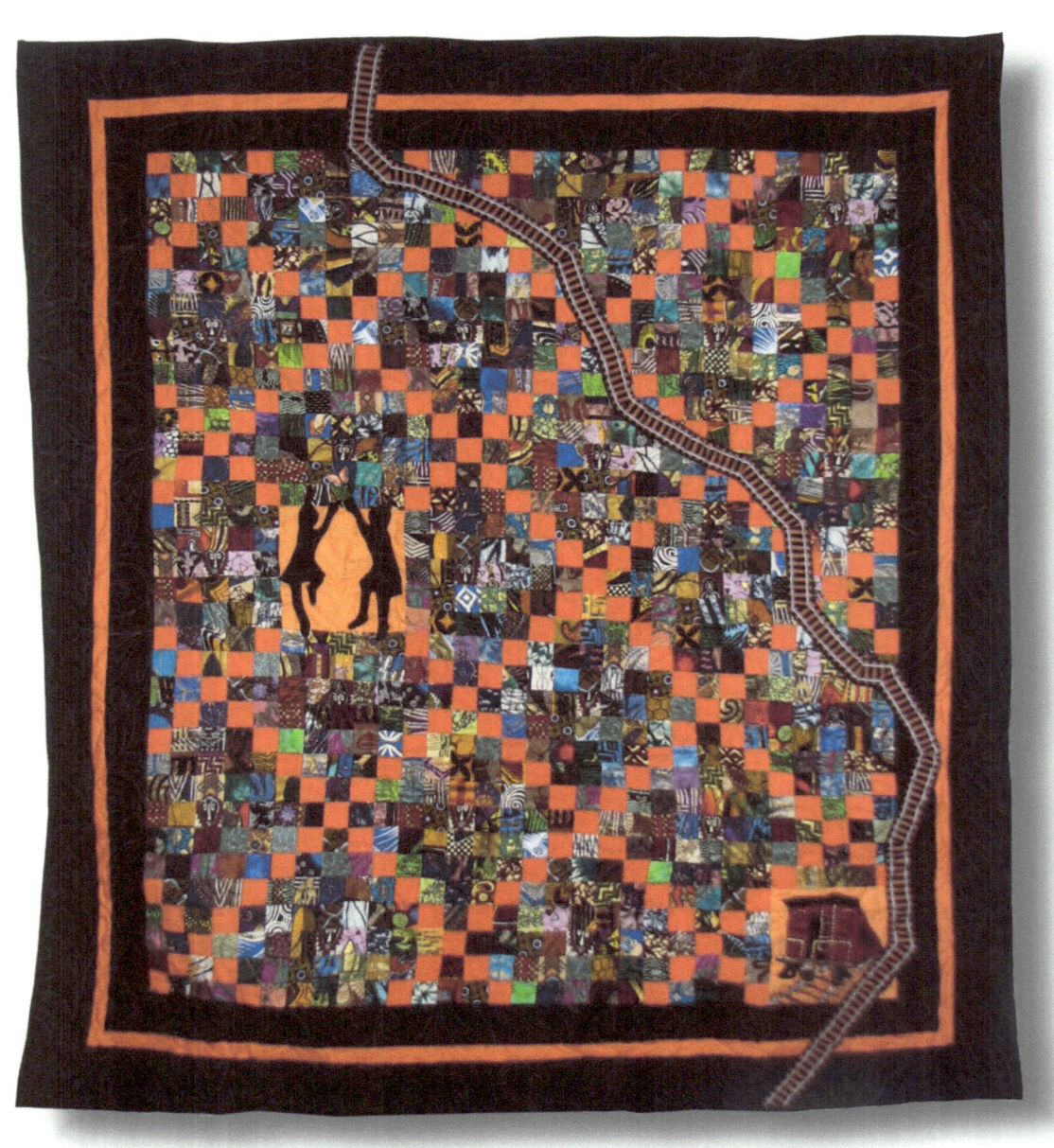

Country Railroad
56" x 63"
2008

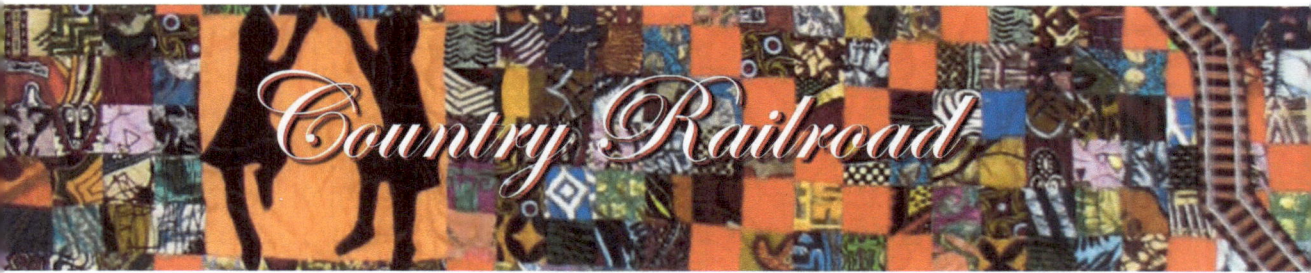

I didn't know my life was so sheltered until I was much much older. We lived on our side of the railroad track and took care of almost all our needs there. I only saw people that looked like me and had no idea that other people existed. I remember realizing the difference one day when we went with my Dad to pick up sodas from Ed McGarity. One day, my Dad took us to the doctor and I saw signs that said Colored in the waiting area. We sat on a long wooden bench against the wall and when the door swung open to the other side of the office; I could see a large potted plant and soft comfortable chairs.

Choo-Choo-chuga chuga chuga chuga choo-choo--------
Cynthia and I would take off across the street and behind the store. Right to the edge of the yard, high on the small hill overlooking the railroad, we'd see the train. "That's my brown car," I'd say. "I call green, I call green," Cynthia would exclaim. We'd stand there, call colors, and claim cars for the length of the train. Each one of us was plotting to be the first to spot the caboose and call it.

Train tracks in America stretch over 30,000 miles. The first tracks were laid in 1826. Now they are a consistent part of the landscape. Tracks enabled America to touch itself, even in the most remote place.

We lived close to the railroad and the horn became an integral part of the background melody. Stories about the railroad were often told.

One such story was told by my sister, Clara. She used to ride with Uncle Troy across the railroad when she was a little girl. She gets tickled as she remembers him flying across the track in his old Chevy and saying, "look quick baby because I don't have time to stop." I could see that childlike excitement still in her eyes.

Next came my sister Cynt's railroad. Griffin was the closest large town to us. Every time we drove there and crossed the railroad, someone in the family would say that's Cynt's railroad. One day I couldn't stand not knowing any longer, so I said why is this Cynt's railroad? As far as I could remember everything was mine and Cynt's. I didn't have a railroad.

"Well," my brother Juan cranked up, "Mama had had seven of her children at home under the watchful eye of a midwife. In 1957 colored people could go to the back door of the Griffin hospital. The hospital had a whole black wing on the back. Mama was having her eighth child in the hospital. Daddy was happy to be going to the hospital because she had lost one at home. When he got to the track, the train was stopped across it. Mama was in labor, so Dad got out of the car and walked the length of the train. 'Mr. Conductor, my wife is about to have her baby and I need to get to the hospital in Griffin,' he said as humble as he could. 'Is there any way possible for you to move the train?' The conductor moved the train and we dubbed it Cynt's railroad because she was almost born there."

One day we heard a loud commotion that shook the whole town. Cynthia and I were scheming on our next adventure. Everybody on my street came out looking to the railroad. People started scurrying in the direction of the train. The sound didn't come from the crossing near us, if it had Ms. Alberta Sims and Eli Patrick would have been the first to know since their houses were close to the railroad crossing. The accident must have happened at the crossing near the church. Word traveled fast in a small town. Friends and neighbors started coming by to say that the train had turned over and we'd better hurry down there. "Hurry, hurry," they all said.

My sister, LaVern headed that way with long rushed steps. Cynt and I ran behind, begging to go. Finally she said, "okay come on." When we got there people were all over the place and so were the contents of the train. The whispers confirmed that no one was hurt in the commotion. We could see Seid Slaughter sitting on his porch watching over the commotion. Someone said he had already got a lot of stuff before the authorities got there. It was Thanksgiving time and the ground was littered with turkeys and hams. The authorities limited the number of turkeys and hams we could take. "Only one per family," they said. Cynt and I were too young and too frail to carry one but LaVern got us one. And the very next day we got word that Seid Slaughter was selling turkeys. I suspect people who'd never had turkey for Thanksgiving were blessed with a turkey that year.

Eli's junkyard was down by the railroad, right in front of his house. My Dad said that hobos lived in those discarded train cars. They would jump trains and go to the next city or town from there. We were warned to say away from that part of the railroad. I was always curious to know the mysteries of the junkyard and the railroad. I couldn't figure out how anyone lived in a junkyard. Every time I walked by, I stretched my neck trying to get a glimpse of one of the hobos. That junkyard and the railroad were fertile ground for many of my imagined escapades.

I often asked myself, why does the train moan so? Chuga chuga chuga chuga choo----- as if it's old bones ached with arthritis. It must have painful memories of stories told to it by the railroad tracks. When you are close to the train you can hear them whispering to each other - swish swish swish - as the cars rock by. I think I know what they are whispering about. The track is telling the train about things it has witnessed.

The way I see it that railroad track has two jobs. The first job is to lay there so the train can reach its destination. The second job was to stand as the racial divide between the black and white communities of rural towns in the southern United States. That racial divide job is slowly changing, but it still stands. She likes whispering the most. That wasn't really her job but something she took up on her own. Swish swish swish

I don't know why stuff happens down by the railroad track, but it does. Down by the railroad. I bet that's why that Train moans so in the distance. Choo-wooo-chuga chuga chuga Chooo. My Uncle JT was killed down by the railroad. Something about two white men and selling some liquor. I never did get the straight of that story because it was always told in hush tones. Malcolm X's father was killed on the railroad. You know he worked with the organization that Marcus Garvey built, U.N.I.A. Papa Step was killed down by the railroad too. Don't know exactly why. We can't really count the deaths that occurred down by the railroad? After all, it was the dividing line.

"That's my red car."
"I call the blue, I call blue," Cynthia would exclaim. I looked down the long row of cars and felt much pain, touching 30,000 miles. I could hear Choo-wooo-chuga chuga chuga in the distance. Then Cynt said, "the caboose, I call the caboose." I said, okay; beat you back to the store.

19

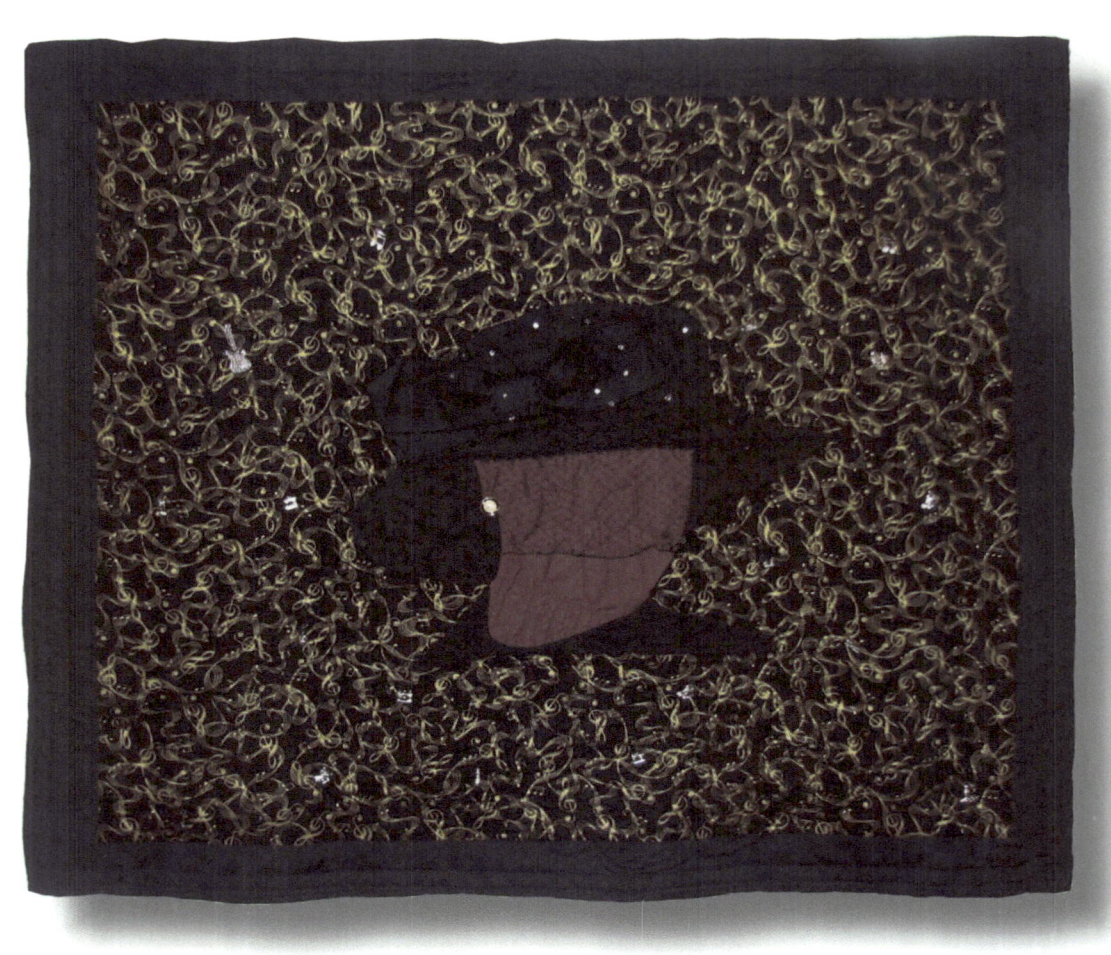

Evening Song
47" x 41"
2006

Evening Song

Aunts (and Uncles) are really important people in a young person's develop-
ment. I had so many aunts that they couldn't all be an integral part of my
life, but the ones that were had a profound effect. Summer vacations at Aunt
Marie's and Uncle Doc's house were so very special.

Aunt Marie tucked us in for the night. She hesitated as she turned off
the light, probably secretly praying that we wouldn't pee the bed. I
turned slightly and the plastic under the sheet crinkled. I quietly
prayed that we wouldn't pee the bed, but we always peed the bed. So
neither of us was surprised in the morning ---both disappointed.

My sister and I cleaned ourselves up and rushed out to breakfast. I
smelled the biscuits while we were in the bathroom. I loved biscuits
and Auntie knew it. She would make two large pans--- one for the
family and one for me. I think she enjoyed watching me eat myself silly.

Auntie moved us along from one thing to the next. I got a chance to
apprentice with her after we finished the breakfast dishes. My sister
Cynthia was only interested in playing outside. I, on the other hand,
was ready and eager to learn to sew.

I wanted to sew like Auntie. She must have seen that desire in me as
well as that impetuousness that pushed my little spirit. That's
probably why she assigned me to the ironing board. I had the auspi-
cious job of trimming the patterns and ironing the seams. It was a long
time before she let me near that sewing machine. I was amazed at how
much I learned about sewing from that ironing board.

My dad's brother Uncle Doc would come home and take us for a walk
around the corner. We'd stop at the corner store to buy ice cream cones.
Sometimes he would buy a half gallon of ice cream at the grocery store
for us. Lemon custard was my absolute favorite flavor. I eventually
became an "Auntie" and took my cues from Aunt Marie. I fashioned
myself as some sort of teacher to my nieces and nephews.

I went by to see Auntie and Uncle Doc whenever I could. I thought Auntie was the greatest when it came to making things. She could make anything, I thought. I went by one day and she was making house slippers for all her grandchildren. On the next visit she was learning to upholster furniture. My wide-eyed amazement never ceased at her talents. Then she learned to macrame' and whoa. That little anxious learning girl from my childhood came out in me. I wanted to make one. So, Auntie gave me some jute and showed me a few knots. Off I went with my homework.

I returned about a week later with my work in tow. I laid it on the sofa in the den. She came in and admonished me for moving her work. I protested that it was mine. She said, "it can't be." She marched right into her sewing area only to find hers still lying where she'd left it. She apologized. It didn't matter to me; my feelings had not been hurt as a matter of fact I was standing there in ecstasy. My work was so good that my teacher could not tell mine from hers.

I always saw her as Auntie, a great seamstress, an exquisite crafter, my teacher and my cousins' mom. I didn't notice that she was a wife, too.

Shortly after Uncle Doc died, my eyes let me see her in a much different light. I went by to visit. We'd both past the stage of teacher/student. It's funny how time eventually lets you become friends. I causally asked how she was doing. Mostly because of training and genuinely because I wanted to know.

Auntie said, "I'm good when I can remember he's gone. It's the days that I cook breakfast and call him in to eat, then walk to the bedroom to see why he didn't come; that's when it's hard. I turned my eyes away so that I would not reflect that sadness back to her. I didn't see Auntie at that moment, I saw a woman who loved a man and had lost him. It was as if she was singing her evening song and I was privy to it.

I quickly stood up and said, "Did you make my biscuits today." She hesitated as she got up probably secretly praying that one day I'd find the kind of love she had had. I turned towards the kitchen and quietly prayed that one day I'd find that kind of love in my life.

If she could see me now – neither of us would be disappointed.

22

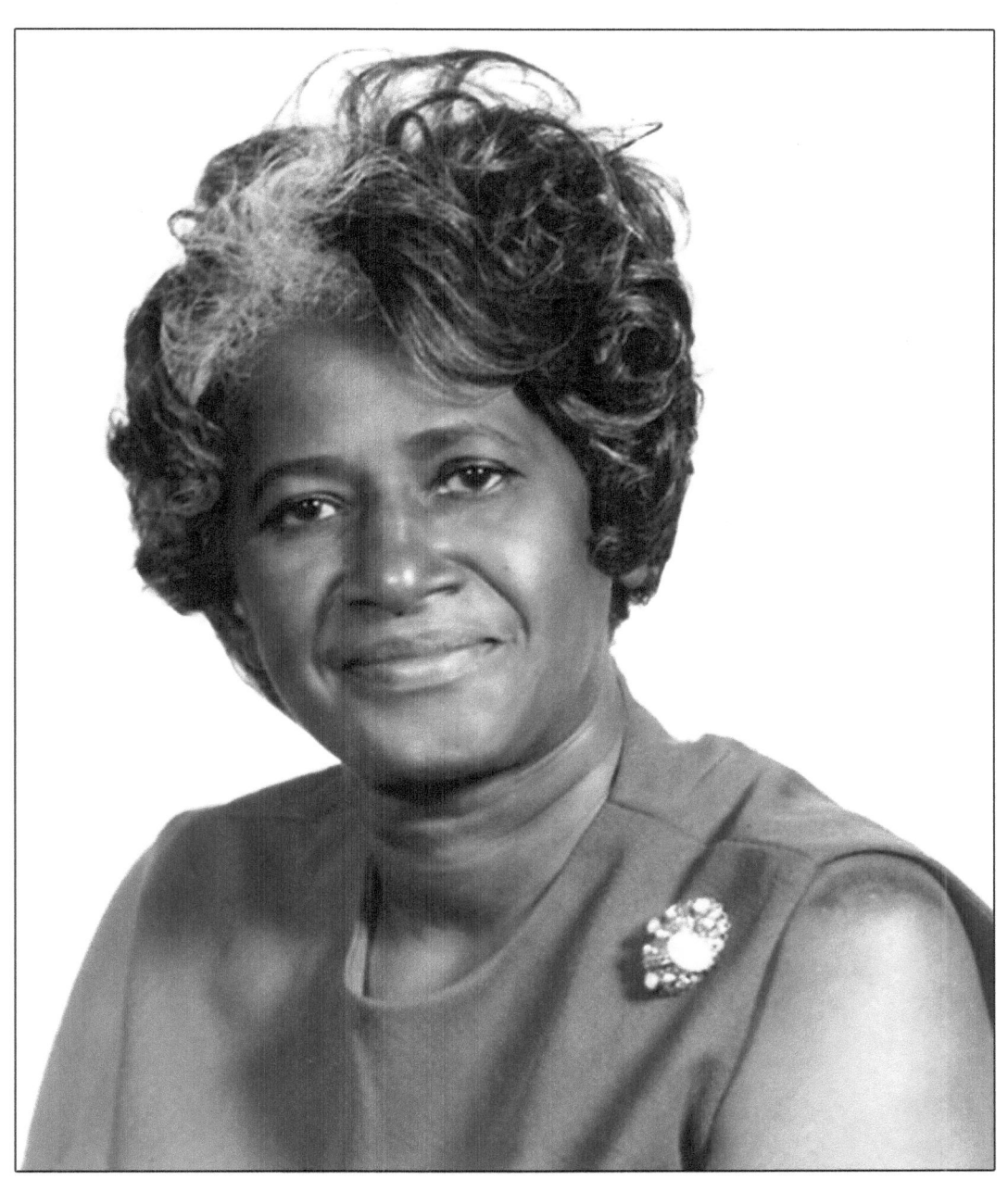

Marie Carmichael Ponder

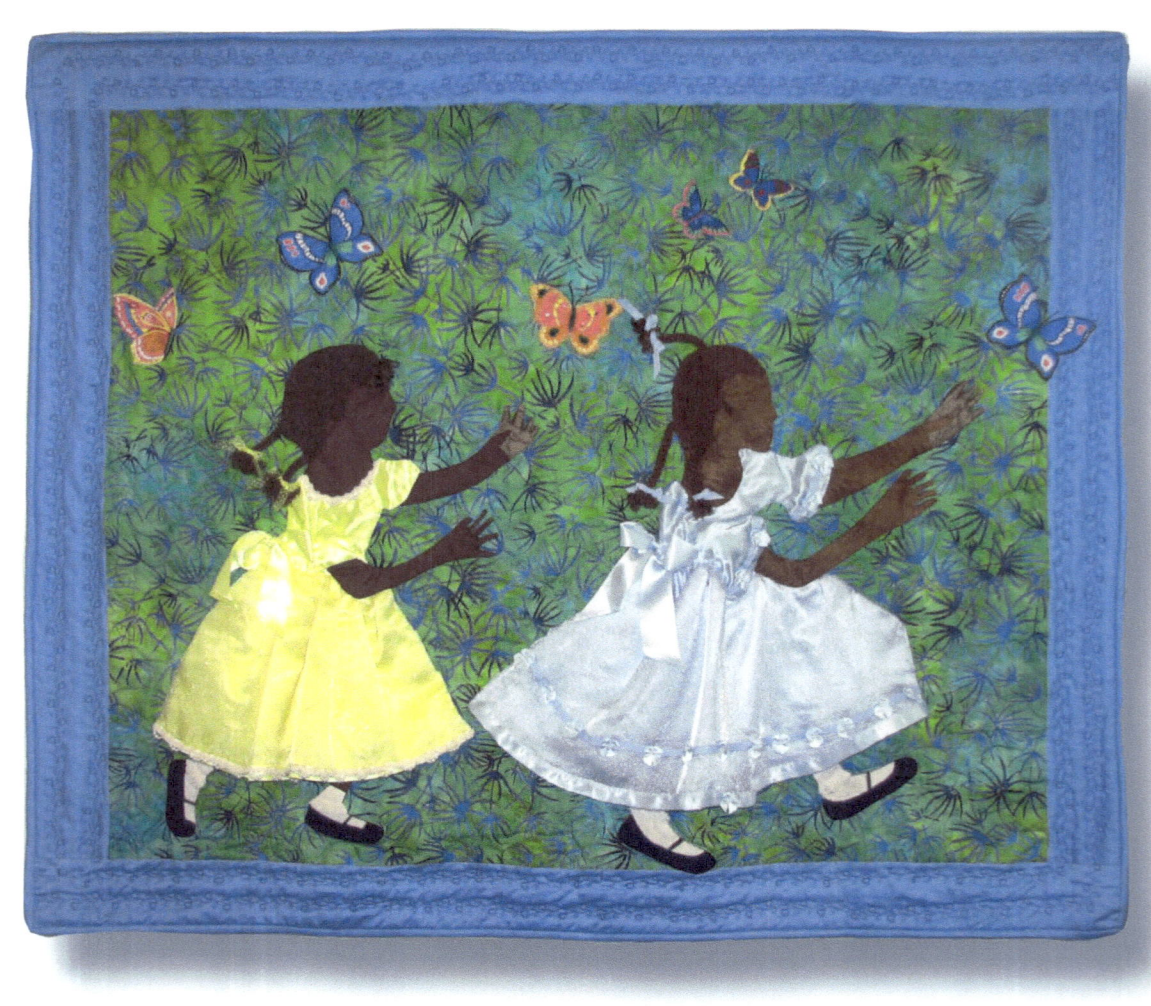

Simple Play
42" x 49"
2009

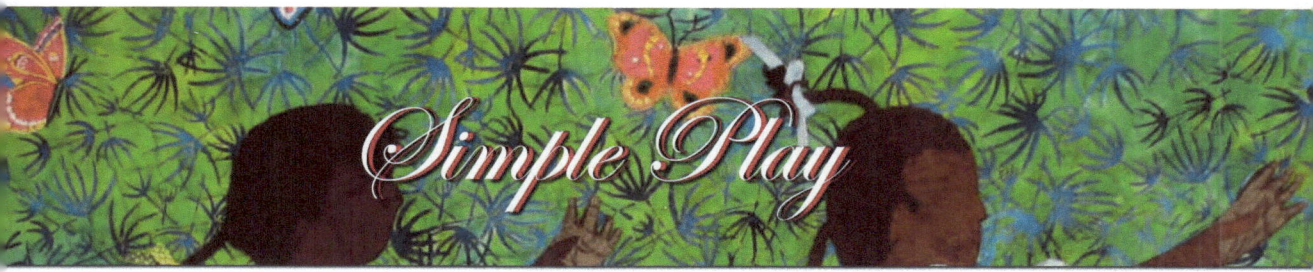

Easter Sunday was a highlight for many little African American girls in the rural south. It was the one day of the year that a special dress, special hair and special occasion meant that you were special. A time for us to be special was so often missing in our lives, that any little change made us smile, sing, run and play.

Who knows why we lock away pictures in the safe recesses of our minds. And who knows how the decision to release them is made. The image of me and Cynt escaped from that special place in my mind where my sister and I live forever as little girls chasing butterflies.

It all started during "Vacation Bible School." Everything was leading up to Easter Sunday and Easter speeches. LaVern took us to the church on Monday morning and many of our friends had arrived before us. The day started with Bible lessons that would end by lunchtime. Lunch must have been pretty non-descript because I don't remember anything about it. Did they serve it there or did we bring a bag lunch?

It was all about the Easter speeches after lunch. That's what I remember most. The grown-ups poured over books filled with poems. They would chop poems at appropriate lengths to match the age and memory capacity of the reciting child. Then they would send us home with a cheery reminder to "Go home and practice." I don't remember Bible study after that first day. It seems that the rehearsals for Sunday's program consumed the week.

Everything was practically the same at home. Then one day, we went shopping. We usually went shopping twice a year, back to school and Easter. We were guaranteed a frilly new dress at Easter time. The kind we only got once a year. LaVern took us to the only two stores in town that were sure to have Easter dresses and that also were the only two that welcomed coloreds. It was good to have her as the "boss of us", because she knew just what to do. When we entered the store, my eyes focused on the perky pink dress on display. I ran over and reached for that same pink dress on the table. As my little hand reached for the dress, LaVern's hand swooped down gently on top of mine. She told me that we didn't want the pink one. Hmm... I did, but she was the boss, so I put it back. LaVern promptly picked out identical dresses in different colors. She always dressed us as if we were twins.

The ride to the Sock Factory in Griffin added even more excitement. I can't quite remember how we got there since LaVern didn't drive. It wasn't really the sock factory but the outlet store next door to the sock factory, where they sold irregulars at bargain prices. I remember wondering where they made the socks in a factory filled with display tables. Irregulars were regulars to us, because that is all we ever had. We each got a new slip, underwear and socks. Ten pairs of socks cost a dollar. LaVern knew a bargain when she saw one, but Cynt and I wanted the baby doll socks. The socks that everyone else wore, but they were 50 cents a pair. LaVern recounted the money and gave us a slow okay. We danced around the store. We didn't dance long because LaVern quickly reined us in. It didn't take much to make us happy.

Sunday morning was abuzz with us happily dressing for the performance. First we'd have to sit through church service, and then the Easter program would immediately follow. Some families skipped church and came just in time for the program. I secretly wanted that.

We were lined up in order of performance on the Deacon's benches. As we sat there fidgeting, I felt the tingle of the burn on my ear. My mind flashed back to the day before when I was on the floor at Ms. Henrietta's house. Ms. Henrietta said, "Sit back in the chair. I won't burn you again." The smell of rose oil pomade drifted past my nose. She always used rose oil pomade when she straightened our hair. I wished I could believe that she wouldn't burn me again. But I knew I was going to flinch every time I felt the heat of that straightening comb close to my neck and she was going to catch my ear again with that hot comb. It never failed. And what was all that burning and ducking for? It was surely a conspiracy to ruin my Saturday. I was not allowed to play after the hair pressing for fear that my hair would go back. The biggest play day of the week and I had to sit still. It made no difference because my hair always went back. I think my hair longed to express its' African roots, consequently it never stayed straightened.

One thing puzzled me, though. I was probably too young to be bothered by such a puzzle, but I was none-the-less. I was always thinking about things that the grown people said. They said that Jesus raised Lazarus from the dead. That statement was so puzzling to me. Well, I thought; my mother was dead. Why didn't He raise her? Was there something special I needed to do?

My feet dangled off the pew and I clicked my patent leather shoes together. I heard them call my name. It was my turn. I went up the steps, curtsied like I'd been taught and projected my voice.

"I never knew my mother
Some folks say she was sweet
But until we meet again
My memory won't be complete."

I bowed. The thunderous clapping surprised me. I did a good job. Pretty soon everybody had their say and it was over. Cynthia and I couldn't wait to leave. The walk home was fun. We relaxed and let the red dirt dust our shiny shoes as we ran. All we could think about was playing as we chased butterflies along the way home. Nothing was sweeter than simple play.

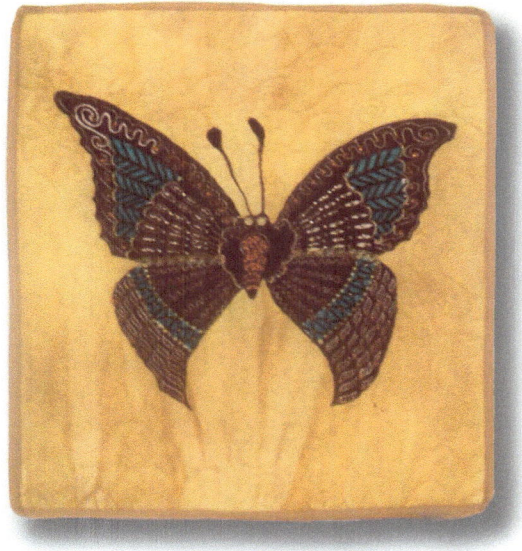

Elusive
2010

27

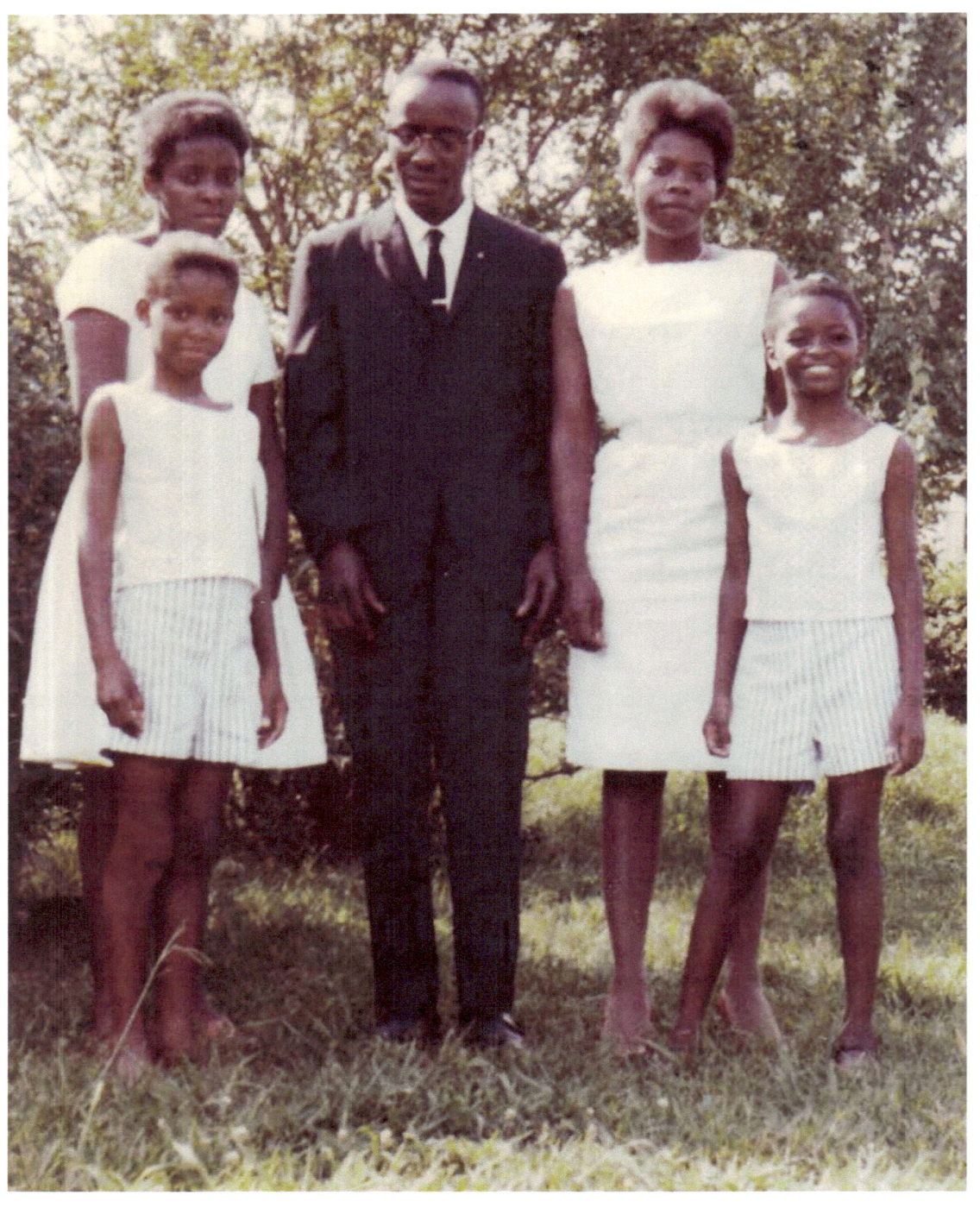

Back Row: Clara P. Wright, Joe D. Ponder, T. LaVern Thomas
Front Row: Aisha Lumumba and Cynthia P. Laster

28

The Making of "If Quilts Could Talk"

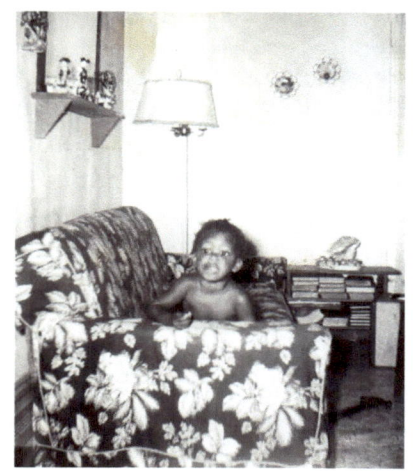

Aisha Lumumba

I forever seem to find myself answering artist calls, especially those I discover online. A lady quilter was penning a book about the process of becoming a quilter. She issued an artist call to other quilters to write a short story about how or why they started to quilt and/or who influenced them. I hurriedly began jotting down some thoughts and memories. I also did a little background research on the history of quilts and the quilting process. I thought long and hard about *why* I started quilting. After thinking I had pinpointed the exact moment that I wanted to quilt, my attention shifted to figuring out who was influential in my pursuit of quilting. Immediately my thoughts captured a visual of Aunt Marie, who taught me to sew.

My short story began with ramblings about the history of quilting and my love of it, and at some point I realized I was no longer writing about quilts, but about someone who had influenced me all of my life. And to my surprise, it was my father, Joe Ponder! It was cathartic! I had not realized the profound effect he had on my life; the love, the lessons, the wisdom, the foundation he had provided, as well as his OWN stories. Wow! I had really taken him for granted all of these years. I finished and submitted my little story about Daddy before the deadline and impatiently awaited the reply. Finally, a nice little note arrived one day, explaining that it was not what they were looking for. Oh, well. I quietly, solemnly tucked my mini tribute away.

So now, I guess you might be wondering how that little story, packed away out of sight, might have blossomed into a full-fledged book. Well, it all started when my Aunt Esther's (my mother's baby sister) family planned a big celebration in South Carolina honoring her 80th birthday. I was there. I love my relatives and relish any opportunity to attend one. We were at my cousin Andrietta's ("Dret" is Esther's second oldest daughter) house, laughing and having our usual good time. Folk were all over Dret's house. Some of the older relatives gathered inside, while another group slipped out the back door where the alcohol was being *discreetly* shared. And the children were out playing games in front giving the teens time to plot their own get-a-way.

One of my many cousins, Marc, started to tell me how he had seen my novel, **Afterwhile**, mentioned on the television show, "Reading Rainbow." If you are familiar, you know that nearing the conclusion of this show, children come forth to tell about a book they have read. Marc continued his story, telling me that a young girl had read **Afterwhile** and he found himself excitedly exclaiming to his friend, "That's my cousin. That's my cousin's book."

Marc then commented to me, "Why don't you write a book about our family?" I smiled a gracious, appreciative smile but deep inside, the thought of committing such to paper *terrified* me. What would I write about? Scandal and violence? Sex and drugs? Those seemed to be the only things selling. Sure, we had our share of scandal, I thought. My own life had a few scandals, but I didn't want to write more of the same. The world already had more than enough of its share of tales about failure, corruption, confusion and the like. Plus, I certainly didn't want to be the one accused of family treason for airing our dirty laundry and getting put out of the family circle!

But there was something unusual about Marc's inquiry. It struck a chord that resonated deeply within me and just wouldn't go away. So after wrestling with the idea for a while, I decided to start chronicling the wonderful, positive stories I remembered about my family. My first story was about my cousin Raynor at Aunt Esther's birthday celebration. "Ray" as we all called him, was Esther's middle son. I felt so good about the way the story turned out that I shared the rough draft with his sister, Mary. I hadn't seen Ray in such a long time. He and I had been close when I first moved away from home on my own. I was happy to see him and glad to have reconnected with him.

That same year, November brought family together again – at my mother's baby brother James' funeral in South Georgia. Although it was a sad occasion, I was elated to see everyone. Ray was there and I was pleased to see him again. We went from not seeing each other for years to twice in one year. Sadly and unexpectedly, four months later, I was on my way to South Carolina to attend Ray's own funeral. Ray had died of heart attack. We hadn't really been in touch the preceding months, which was so disappointing. I had the awesome pleasure of traveling to his homegoing celebration with all three of my brothers and their wives, but that's another story. When we got there, much to my surprise, family members were remarking how much they enjoyed my story about Ray. Mary had circulated the story amongst relatives. It was a rewarding feeling that other people, especially family, had enjoyed the story.

At one point during the gathering, Ray's younger brother Stacey came over looking mysteriously at me as if I had done something magical and if he looked closely enough, he'd be able to see the trick mirrors. He said, "Did you videotape Ray during Mama's birthday party?" He looked at me suspiciously and moved closer as if his eyes were saying "no sudden moves, I'm watching you." I replied, "No." He said, "Well I did and your story was verbatim. How did you do that?" I had to confess that I have somewhat of a photographic memory. He said, "Oh okay," but he walked away, still looking somewhat puzzled combined with an air of skepticism.

Ray's funeral marked the real beginning of my **positive** family storytelling. Ray's story will appear in a future volume of **If Quilts Could Talk**. When the annual Decatur (Georgia) Arts Festival time came, Jerry G. White asked me to perform. At the time, I only had two stories: the newer one about Cousin Ray and the first one about my Dad, that I had put away after its nice rejection. But Jerry G. said that he needed a twenty-minute performance. Twenty long minutes! So I put on my thinking cap and wrote "Evening Song." I struggled a little with that story because I wanted it to be all positive, but it also dealt with some unhappiness. I didn't want to write a whole lot of sad stories, but it wouldn't be the same story had I omitted the sorrow. I am no theatrical performer but when I finished, the crowd stood and applauded. They came up to me afterwards to tell me how the stories affected them. And at that moment, I knew a book was about to be born.

As I look over my life, I find niches filled with nuances of gestures, sayings, and habits that create a colorful palette, a masterpiece interwoven by threads of family memories, rich history and cultural traditions. I've heard it said, that everyone has a story, but not everyone is afforded the chance to tell their story - her story or his story. I am so thankful to be telling my side of it - my story. And if my quilts could talk, the stories they would tell, would tell it all.

31

About The Author

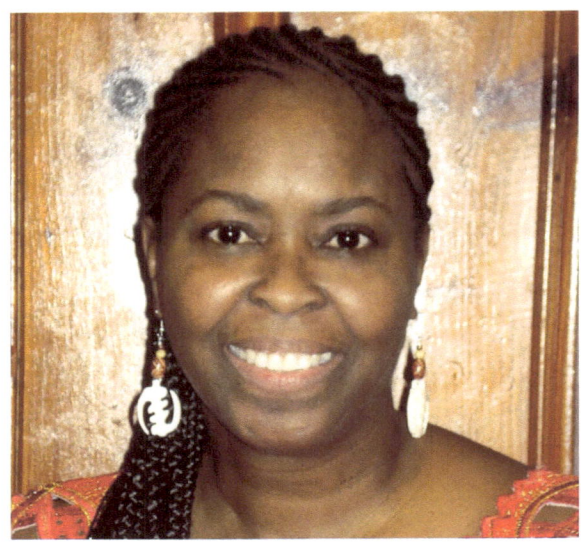

Aisha Lumumba is a fiber artist, who now lives in Atlanta, Georgia. She started exhibiting quilts in 1983. Her quilts have appeared in more than thirty-five exhibits throughout the United States. Ms. Lumumba is available for Art Exhibits, Lectures, Quilt-Story Telling, Classes, Workshops, and Trunk Shows.

Aisha loves sewing, quilting, writing, and cooking. She is a well-known vegan cook and is famous among friends and family for her biscuits.

Other Titles by Aisha Lumumba
Gifted: Art Quilts featuring African American History Makers
Afterwhile: The Secrets of a Woman's Heart
Cuisine on the Nile Volumes 1 and 2

www.obaquilts.com for more Art Quilts

www.ingramcontent.com/pod-product-compliance
Lightning Source LLC
Chambersburg PA
CBHW050411180526
45159CB00005B/2230